Beyond The Pale

Beyond The Pale

A collection of poems

by Jana Synková

With pen & ink illustrations
by Isabella Synek Herd

With thanks to Isabella Synek Herd

All poems are the copyright property of
Jana Synková
2021

All illustrations, including
front cover illustration,
are the copyright property of
Isabella Synek Herd

A CIP record for this book
Is available from the British Library

ISBN 979-849 034 4681

To Richard,
With love.

CONTENTS

V   The Extraordinary Ordinary

VI   Final Word

Introduction

Beyond the Pale is my second collection of poems. The title
was chosen, not on account of Anglo/Irish history ('The Pale',
referring to a strip of land under English rule in late-medieval
Ireland, fenced off by 'pales', or stakes, beyond which the 'free
Irish' deemed dangerous and unruly, dwelt) although there *is* an
Irish link (*In the Emerald Isle's/Verdant pastures -/Lands
blessed/With poetry*...see Part V*)*, but rather, on account of the
pictures the idiom conjures up, both literal and metaphorical,
and the various levels at which it invites interpretation.

Besides its more pejorative connotations, covered by the
darker poems, a less usual meaning is also lent to it here: a
breaking away from the pale and the ordinary in favour of the
vibrant and the extraordinary. Somewhat vindicating the Irish?
In *Final Word,* 'beyond the pale' can refer to a societal or
political situation which has gone too far as well as to the moral
and intellectual, if not literal, exile imposed upon the lucid or
the principled.

I have included *The Memory of Walls* from my first
collection, since the significance of the childhood home and the
phenomena of nostalgia and memory, are all things that I
continue to write on – a subject-matter which deserves to be
amplified by the eloquence of expression which poetry allows.
Whilst all of these poems embody varying degrees of
wistfulness, the darker aspects (e.g. *The Brambles*) are
compensated for by more positive elements (*The Doves*).

The Parts of this collection otherwise differ somewhat from
the first: instead of *Fauna & Flora*, we find *Natural &
Unnatural States* (Part I)*,* which emphasizes both the fragility
and the power of nature. Apart from *Woodlands in Autumn*, and
Cruel Sea (the latter, borrowed from the first collection), these
are slightly longer or otherwise narrative-style poems; whereas
Part II (Landscape, Seascape, Skyscape) also covers natural
themes, but with more lyricism and brevity.

Matters of Life and Death (Part III) includes metaphysical
questions about earthly existence, the human condition, and
speculation about what lies beyond. Apart from an old
favourite, *Quintessence of Dust,* these are all new poems,
unpublished elsewhere.

Those who have read my first collection, which includes
Blue, how I love you Blue! inspired by Garcia Lorca's

celebrated *Green, how I want you, Green!* will notice that, in spite of an intention not to do so, I have succumbed to the self-indulgence of writing a poem inspired by the latter (see Part V, *The Extraordinary Ordinary*) - not a patch on Lorca's of course, but in my own defence, it *is* very much a favourite colour and the poem differs almost entirely in subject-matter, so I hope I will be forgiven.

Part V, on the whole, lauds those small details of our everyday surroundings and lives, too often taken for granted; the simple but striking or meaningful things which, as it happens, lend themselves to poetry so perfectly.

I very much hope that you will enjoy this collection of poems as much as the first. Excerpts from some of my current writings can be seen in my Book Room, linked to from **@blackbirdsandme (Instagram).**

Jana Synková

I
NATURAL AND UNNATURAL STATES

There is no forgiveness in nature

- Ugo Betti

UNNATURAL
STATES

I

Wild hearts,
Beat fast,
In tiger'd stripes,
Zebra brights,
Camouflage:
Run, hide, survive.
Last strongholds
From savanna to Sumatra,
Amazon forest
To Boreal,
Pole to Pole,
Fading fast.
Until the last
Will be seen
Through walls of glass
And the iron bars
Of zoological parks;
And in stately homes
In private collections
Of stuffed heads
Mounted on
Wood-panelled walls:
Sport and spoils
Of the privileged classes
At the height
Of 'civilization'.

II

Meanwhile,
In the wilds
Of concrete jungles,
Urban decay thrives,
Amidst graffiti-
Marked territory
Ruled by
Fear and rivalry:
Run, hide, survive.
Young lives
In jeopardy
Trapped by poverty,
In great cities
Without pity.

Nature is cruel
They say;
But how much more so
Is cruelty man-made,
Fuelled by greed
Or ignorance,
Indifference,
Hatred.
Civilization
Losing its grip;
Lost futures of those
Born in lands of plenty
As masks slip;
Loose ends, swept
Under the carpet.
Great chasms
Between
Those who have
And haven't.
Hope fading fast
In the ghetto
- No exit.

III

As for those who seem
To have it all:
Scratch the surface
And see how quickly
Joy crumbles
In gilded cages
And closed-in spaces.
How the bored mind
Races;
The unfulfilled heart,
Rages;
The restless body,
Paces.

When, on Earth,
Did the pursuit
Of happiness
Become so fruitless?

IV

The call of the wild
Beckons at first
With a small voice
Scarcely heard;
But if listened to,
Beneath the deafening
Din of modernity,
It becomes a lion's roar –
A yearning for
The valleys and woods
Of youth;
The mountains and shores
Of forefathers;
The adventurous spirit
Of explorers before us:
A primal urge;
An instinct.

And in these dreams
Of escape,
Castles in Spain
Do not figure:
Rather, the plain
Homely wood cabin
Of the forest dwelling,
Or the humble
Stone building
Of the crofter
Making an honest
Living:
Four walls; a roof;
A fire; fresh water:
Self-sufficiency;
Simplicity;
A tight-knit
Community.

Looking to the past
For a lost happiness
In the wilds,
Untamed,
Magnificent and vast;
If it's not too late.

Run, fast
Wild hearts!

THE GREAT STORM OF 1987

Something in the air
Signalled a warning.
A small,
Barely perceptible
Change:
A bristling of hair,
A feeling…
That eerie calm
Before a storm
Which speaks in
Its unnatural
Stillness.

But the weather forecaster*
Never foresaw disaster.
Smiling dismissively
He exclaimed,
Someone reckons
A hurricane is on its way!
Words which would return
To haunt him to this day.

Our house on a hill
Stood like a rock,
As brick-built
Buildings
Of its era will.
But the pines trees
Swayed
A little more
Than usual
In the breeze
That evening,
And Dad looked out
And said,
I don't like it -
Something is afoot!

So he was to decide
That all should retire,
To the other side
Of the house that night;
And that is the night
The hurricane came.

And it came
With an almighty
Vengeance,
The likes of which
Had not been seen
In this country
For three centuries.
And the tall pines
Fell on the house
Like ten-pins.

And all about
The countryside
And in grand town parks
With specimen plantings,
Ancient trees:
Sycamores, oaks
Redwoods,
Were uprooted;
Bent; shattered;
Strewn across roads,
Railways, streets,
As in some
Apocalyptic scene.

These local happenings
Were reported to me
Later on;
For at the time,
I was an undergraduate
In London,
Before the days of internet
And mobile phones;

And from my digs
In Queen Elizabeth Hall**
I heard not a thing.
But I went for a stroll
The next morning
With my friend Gail,
Down Campden Hill
To Kensington Gardens,
Quite unsuspecting -
To be met with
The absurd spectacle
Of huge trees upended,
Roots, exposed as
Grotesque tentacles.

The storm
Was indiscriminate.
Young saplings and
Great-girthed giants alike
Were susceptible
To topple or tumble -
High or humble.
In Kensington Gardens
It was the Jubilee Walk,
An avenue of lime trees,
Which bore the brunt
Of casualties.

At Sevenoaks,
A single oak remained
To the town's name -
The devastated land
Where the storm
Had laid siege,
Resembling
The aftermath of war.
The local paper
Summed it up
In their headline,
Our Darkest Hour.

Coastal areas
Were hard hit
By the weather bomb:
Overnight,
Boats capsized;
Caravans
On cliff-top sites
Were tipped
Onto their sides;
And the old wood pier
At Shanklin
On the Isle of Wight
Was reduced to flotsam.

Back at our place:
A gash in the roof
And the glass
Of a bedroom window,
Smashed,
Where the branches
Crashed through.
My sisters
Had slept fast;
But not our father,
Who faced
An anxious wait
To see the extent
Of the disaster
At daybreak,
When the storm
Was over.

Now the work began
Up and down
The land:
Repairing roofs
And window panes;
Mending power lines;
Insurance claims…

And the tall pines,
A defining feature
Of our property,
Were destined
For firewood
And kindling;
A lone tree,
Silhouetted against
A desolate sky;

The last
Left standing.

** Queen Elizabeth Hall was a hall of residence on Campden Hill
Road, attached to the Queen Elizabeth College campus, which by then
(since 1985) was merged with King's College London. The campus
was closed and sold in the year 2000, and the buildings have
subsequently been re-developed.

The Ballad
Of the WILD CATS

Ours were no ordinary cats!
Raised to be half-wild,
They were 'kept'
To kill mice and rats;
But in reality,
There was no keeping them:
They lived
At their own behest,
These magnificent beasts.

They came
Without names,
But they were tabbies,
Of course,
Complete with the stripes
Any self-respecting tiger
Would sport.
So 'Tiger' it was
For the lass,
Whilst the tom,
For reasons quite obvious,
We called 'White Paws'.

Great was the excitement
When the 'big cats'
Arrived.
But they hissed
And snarled
In their boxes-with-
Breathing-holes;
And scrambled
And tore
When emptied into
The shed
By the paddock,
For their settling-in period.

In the early days,
If you peeped round the door
Of their sleeping place,
They would skulk
In a corner,
With hackles raised.
But over time,
They grew less afraid,
And were free to roam.
Each morning, I'd take up
A saucepan
Of 'lights' and offal
I'd cooked on the hob -
A squeamish job -
But I was determined
To tame them,
Whatever it took.
They didn't eat
Tinned meat!

They were fed once a day
Lest they might stray;
For the rest,
They were to hunt
And prey,
And they did.
Dad was glad
As mice populations
Went down;
Whilst we were sad
At the odd carcass of rabbit
Found lying around:
The speciality
Of White Paws,
The great roamer
Of the open field.
Tiger's expertise,
Being lazier in habit,
Was as mole-catcher-in-chief
By the vegetable patch:

She'd lie completely prostrate,
One arm down a hole,
Up to her armpit,
In pursuit of a mole,
Waiting for the slightest
Sound or movement -
And then swipe
In a sudden paroxysm
Of killer-instinct.

Of a morning before school,
I'd go up, rain or shine,
Frost or snow,
And bang
With a metal spoon
On that old saucepan
With their food;
Until from far afield,
They came running,
Sometimes separately,
Sometimes, together,
To snatch –
Somewhat ungratefully,
I thought -
The day's easy catch.

By now, Tiger would,
If in the right mood,
Come to you,
For a brief caress;
Whilst White Paws,
More aloof,
Would tolerate affection
Only under duress,
Allowing but a light stroke
Of his glossy coat,
Before darting off
With disdainful
Indignance.

I made the mistake, once,
Of carrying Tiger
Indoors -
(Had I not
 half-tamed her?)
She dug in her claws,
Limbs stiffened in terror,
And flew at the curtains,
Without reckoning on
The voile nets or
Glass window-panes.
By the time
I'd unhooked her,
I was scratched to pieces,
And the experiment
Was never repeated.

A few years after
Their dramatic arrival,
The big cats left.
Without warning or signal.
It just happened that one day
I was banging away
On the old saucepan lid
Up by the shed,
But no cats came.
Not then,
Nor the next day.
The call of the wild,
The nearby woods,
Where they went,
Who can say?

But a part of this story
Is yet to be written:
Some time before this,
Tiger had kittens!
And *their* tale
Must be saved
For another day...

CRUEL SEA

Wild winter sea,
Relentless
Waves lashing;
Pitiless
Grey-green.
Wind-driven
Ripples,
Rolling crests
Of mountainous masses
Crashing.
Devastating storm,
Stirring up debris
From the shore;
Cruel sea,
Cutting cliffs,
Corrosive.
Muddied waters,
Brown with
Rucked-up sandstone;
Dirty foam.
The wind,
A long continuous
Moan.
A slate sky,
Drizzling and dull;
Monotony broken
By the screech
Of a gull.

PLAY-ACTING

Morning drops down
As the curtain rises;
Somewhere,
Off-stage,
The sun is shining.
And in the wings,
Out of sight,
Someone gives
Stage directions,
Pulls the strings.

You put on
Your mask
And say you love me:
Lines you know
By heart.
Still, I must
Congratulate you
On how well
You play
Your part.

You always did
Like to be
Centre-stage;
The lead character
In the play;
The darling
Of the theatre;
The limelight
Ever was
Your element.

And between
The *trompe l'oeil*
Of the scenery
And your plausible
Sincerity,

It is hard
To separate
Make-believe
From reality;
Romance,
From performance;
The truth,
From the lie.

But when night falls,
With a roll
Of drums,
A paper moon
Hangs
In a paper sky.

WOODS
IN LATE AUTUMN

The breeze is gentle
Through the trees,
And if the woods
Could talk,
They'd speak
In brittle whispers
Of rustling leaves,
Like tambourines
With fragile zills
Of tarnished copper;
Ripe seeds
Rattling
In maracas.

Later still,
When winter
Follows,
The high-pitched
Trill
Of wood-wind
Instruments,
Whistles through
The eerie hollow;
And the woods sing
With a shrill
And severed
Voice,
As arms of trees
Are bared,
And the last
Straggling leaves,
Hang
By a thread.

II

LANDSCAPE SEASCAPE SKYSCAPE

Seest thou the sunbeam's yellow glow,
That robes with liquid streams of light;
Yon distant Mountain's craggy brow.
And shows the rocks so fair, - so bright -

- Percy Bysshe Shelley, *Hope*

SLEEPING SEA

Sleeping sea,
How calm you seem,
This night
Without breeze.
Your waves are dreams
Lapping on shores
Of shingle,
Murmuring
In slow,
Somniferous
Ebb and flow.

And looking down,
The moon
Observes
Her opal face
In scattered
Fragments,
On the surface,
As if
Through a glass
Darkly.

Oh,
The inky depths
Dwell
Never more so
In the realms
Of myth
Than in the hush
Of indigo,
Where whispered
Stories,
Carried forth
On tides
From long ago,
Are rocked
In cradles, and
In storm-worn
Boats.

And the sea's
Berceuse
Lulls,
With soulful sighs
And soothing
Verse,
In rageless waters,
Far from
The foreboding
Swell;

Each shallow
Breath,
Barely a wrinkle
In time,
Yet ceaselessly
Eternal,
And divine.

TWILIGHT

Behold the pink
Of the sky
At twilight;
And of the street-lights
Softly stirring.
On the horizon,
Near yet far,
The edges
Of the world
Are blurred,
And melt away
By the half-hour.
Pink turns to mauve,
Then dims to grey.

The sodium-lights,
Now bright,
Switch up
To orange
And embrace
The gathering dark;
Until at last,
The felted cloak
Of night
Is drawn across
The shoulders
Of the globe,
Braced against
The cold.

COLMER'S HILL

There stands
The lonely hill,
Seen from afar
By the traveller
On this stretch
Of the coast road;
A giant, by no means,
Yet so it seems:
Head peeping up
Above its neighbours
With distinctive
Flat-cap,
And top-knot
Of pine trees;
And outfits changing
With the seasons.

In Autumn,
Its sloping shoulders,
Cloaked in bracken,
Turn to amber;
Whilst Winter's
Scattering of snow
Tucks about its chin,
A coat of ermine.
In Spring-time,
Bluebells
In hues of violet
Adorn its forms;
And Summer bestows
Upon its meadows,
Verdant folds
Of velvet.

Someday,
Instead of passing through,
I'll climb
That lonely hill
At Symondsbury,
And see
The fabled view
A certain Viking
Took a liking to,
Adding his name
To local
Etymology.

Until then,
I can only imagine
The brilliance
Of shining sea,
And the lush
Of green;
And scattering
Of farms,
And dots of sheep;
And dips of valleys,
And ribbons
Of streams;

And the vista,
Unspoilt still -
In many ways
Little changed
Since Viking days -
Of this corner
Of Dorset,
Old as the hills.

SEATON BEACH

How often
We sat on the stones
Of Seaton beach.
The sandy shores
Further along
The coast, are,
By some,
Loved most;
But we shunned
The crowds
And rowdy scenes,
And edge-to-edge
Beach towels, and
Sand-in-sandwiches.

At the far end,
At Seaton Hole,
It was pleasant
To stroll
On the foreshore
At low tide;
And when the children
Were small,
To potter a while,
Amidst the rockpools,
And curious creatures
Which lurked inside.

On the expanse
Of pebbles,
One could forget,
For a bit,
One's troubles:
Watch as
The ebb and flow
Diminished all
To foam.

Whilst the little folk
Busied themselves,
Sifting through
Innumerable stones;
And splashing in water
So cold,
It drew laughter.

I will never forget
The first time we saw it,
Approached
From down
The steep slope
Of the Chine:
That first burst of blue
Glimpsed through
The great gorge
In the mudstone;
Then on past
The Hideaway café
Overlooking the bay.
The sound of the sea,
Ever closer,
Lapping against
The shore.

The children are now
Quite grown.
But the sea
And its memory
Will, ever more
- I am hopeful -
Like the returning
Tide,
Draw them
Home.

WISH YOU WERE HERE
~A postcard from Seaton

Clean is the air
And crisp,
Yet sheltered
Beneath the cliffs.
If one wishes
To avoid the effort
Of walking on
The pebbles,
The esplanade obliges
With its wide
And level pavement.
And on the stretch
Adjacent to
The Hideaway café,
One could almost be
On the deck
Of an ocean liner,
Looking out to sea.

For Seaton Beach remains
Unspoilt
For the most part:
Ignored by the hordes
Of day-trippers
Skipping blithely past
To Lyme;
Its outlook, unmarred,
By heavy industry;
And its esplanade,
Spared
The tackier aspects
Of larger seaside towns.

Be sure to visit
If you get a chance:
You'll soon succumb
To its small-town
Charms:
The vintage trams
And fish and chips;
Visitor Centre
And restaurants;
Cliff Top Gardens
And labyrinth;
And last
But not least,
Its *pièce de résistance:*
The mile-long beach.

It's no Blackpool
– thankfully,
And there is no pier;
But there are rockpools,
And the views
Are unrivalled.

Don't you wish
You were here?

IN THE DEEP NIGHT

The night sky
Is as the ocean,
Vast;
Deeper than all
Imagining;
Deeper than inky
Seas and fjords;
Deeper than sleep
And dreams
And thoughts.
And in its remote
And twinkling stars
Are other shores
Light years
From ours,
Which shone before
The light we see,
In that strange galaxy
Of waveless seas.

And how its distant fires
Stir the heart
And passions, stoke,
Shining, soulful
In moonless realms
As black as coal;
Burning seams
So fervently aglow,
As if projections
Of our own desires
And hopes,
Reflected in
Those reachless heights,
Far and fathomless
Of starry skies
In deepest,
Darkest,
Nights.

III
MATTERS
OF
LIFE & DEATH

And we are here as on a darkling plain
Swept with confused alarms of struggle and flight
Where ignorant armies clash by night.

- Matthew Arnold, *Dover Beach*

WHY?

Could it be,
If God exists,
That He
Calls soonest
Those held dearest?
What else
Might explain
The oft' early departure
Of those who are
Kindest or best;
Or bravest;
Or purest?

And what if Hell
Were right here,
On earth? Well,
Sometimes
It feels like it,
When days
Are darkest,
And hearts
Are heartless.

Dead poets
And the likes of Sartre
Will know
By now whether
His 'Huis Clos'
L'enfer,
C'est les autres
Applies above,
Or rather,
Here -
Below;

Or whether
A closer translation
Might resemble
Dante's *Inferno*:
Layers of afterlife
To traverse
According to
Just deserts -
All helpfully
Set out in verse.

All the same,
It is hard to view
Without scepticism
The necessity of
The suffering
Of innocents:
But let's assume
They jump the queue.

In the absence
Of certainty,
Therefore,
Best not yet
Slam shut
The door:

For when our time comes,
And the sums
Of accountability
Are done,
We might learn, at last,
Where lies the truth
And where, the lie;
But first,
And foremost,
Why.

QUINTESSENCE OF DUST

No, it surely cannot be
That earth turns round
Indifferently,
And skies,
So full of hidden fires,
Are cold.
It cannot be
That flesh and blood
Are cheap as dirt,
No more than dust.
This breath,
So loath to cease,
Can't heave in vain,
Nor for no reason
Stop
So suddenly;
These thoughts,
This stream
Of consciousness -
Mere nothingness.

For within us
Lies the knowledge,
Buried deep,
Of time long past,
Before the womb,
Which was not void,
Nor sleep,
Of which the vaguest
Consciousness
Remains,
And which will last
Beyond the tomb.

There is a distant echo –
A faint pulse

That's not the beating
Of our hearts
Nor angels' wings.
And souls
Of young and old
Will, one day,
Be free
From earth-bound
Things,
And heaviness,
And harm,
And restless sleep.
And in this world
Of now,
It matters less *how long*,
Than *how*,
With good intent
And grace,
We live our lives
Before
This leap of faith.

LAST CHANCE SALOON

Here,
In the domain
Of the absurd,
My voiceless words
Speak, unheard:
A nightmarish dream
From which no pinch
Wakes me, nor scream.
Hope, dangling
From a string.

I strain to hear,
But the sounds
Are muffled -
Unclear;
Signs,
Indecipherable.
The number you are
Trying to reach
Is unobtainable.

I push the door
Of glass
Through which,
I see,
Others have passed
Easily.
But for me,
It revolves
Endlessly.

Ah, I was always
The black sheep
Of the family;
The square peg
In the round hole;
The head
Above the parapet.

And I have walked
So many miles
Across the desert,
Parched
And unforgiving.
All my life
I have refused
To play the cards
That I was given.
But now,
I am thirsty,
And so very weary.

It is high noon
At the
Last Chance
Saloon;
And I am
On the outside,
Looking in.

NO MILK TODAY

The rain never stops.
It falls in slants
Through window panes:
Wet drops
Through broken glass,
Never replaced.
It's all right.
Cold draughts,
Drive
The damp home;
Chilled to the bone.

A forced smile,
Worn out from wearing,
On lips, slowly frozen;
Inside,
Slowly dying.
I'm fine.

Through the window:
No view,
Just a wall of concrete,
Beyond a street
Of footless footsteps
And faceless figures.
None of them you.

Rain turns to drizzle,
Entrenching misery,
Like a knife to a wound.
Waiting dully
For the phone,
Never ringing,
The note,
Never bringing.

No milk today.

Time stuck,
Unshifting.
Hands on the clock
Slowly ticking.
Numb acceptance
Setting in;
Sifting
Through embers.
I'm okay.
No dust settling,
Only ashes.

The rain never stops.

TORO! TORO!

Piercing
Is the afternoon sun
In the bullrings
Of Andalucía.

Loud are the cheers
From the barreras
As the protagonists
Appear.

Unbearable
Is the tension
As the *Paso Doble*
Rings out,
With inexorable
Rhythm,
Marching to
Destiny's sound.

This is no play,
Nor the theatre:
The stage
Is the scorched dust
Of *albero;*
The curtains,
The cruel capes
Of death.

With bated breath
Wait the spectators,
And the toreros
With heart in mouth,
As the toro
Enters the arena,
And angrily
Paws the ground.

And so the corrida
Unfolds
In the cloths
Of magenta
And gold;
And the final flourish
Of scarlet
In the muleta
The matador holds.

It is a dance
To the death,
Most macabre:
No flamenco,
Nor joyous fiesta
Despite bright-coloured
Banderillos,
It is a tango
Grim and sinister.

Sorrow
Runs in the tears
Of the toro,
And the mothers
Of sons of Spain,
As one life or another
Is taken
In a tradition
Of honour and pain.

For the one who
Leaves not
The arena -
The matador
Or the toro -
The Andalucían sun
Will cease to beat down,
For there will be no
Tomorrow.

IV
THE MEMORY OF WALLS
~Revisited

Only one who loves can remember so well

- Anton Chekhov, Selected Stories

WEEKEND HOUSE

We had a weekend house
In Moravia.
On a tree-topped hillside
Overlooking a reservoir.

Such a thing might seem
An impossible dream
Under a communist
Regime;
But thus it stood,
Solid and real.
Perhaps it was allowed
In order to dispel ill will -
Or to prevent a wanderlust
Further afield -
For part and parcel
Of the Czech way of life
Was the weekend house:
A rural idyll
Away from week-day strife.

The *chata**
Was made of timber
Painted dark brown,
With white render
Half-way down.
Set on a slope
Of meadow grass
Amidst similar others,
It looked just like
The jewellery-box house
Given to me by my father
When I was six
And the scaled-down
Models built
By the Czech uncles
Out of matchsticks.

Pine-clad within
And box-beds,
Built-in,
It catered for
Basic needs
With shelter and larder,
And water, fetched
In a pitcher.
The forest surrounds
Were filled with
The carefree sounds
Of birdsong
And the laughter
Of children,
Free to wander.

On our visit each year
To Moravia,
It was here,
In good weather,
That family
Would gather:
Paddling in the clear
Water of the lake,
(I, with my beloved turtle
Inflatable)
And after,
Retiring to the *chata*
For potato salad,
Dumplings – (knedlíky)
Sweet sauerkraut (zeli)
And Czech cake.

Towards evening,
A lamp of paraffin
Lit the room
As dark crept in,
Amidst the grown-ups'
Animated talk
Around the table

And gesticulations
Which enabled
A half-guessing
At conversations.
The shadows cast
Upon the walls
Grew ever more
Dramatic
With night-fall.
Until gradually,
We became drowsy…
Entranced
By the chatter
And reminiscing,
As midges danced
About the light.

Oh, to spend the night
At the *chata,*
Was the height
Of excitement!
To sleep, tucked up
In those bunks,
Until daylight
Stole in
Uninvited.

Those sun-drenched days
And gloriously
Drawn-out evenings
Remained
In the memory
Long after;
Perhaps never more so
Than for our father,
Whose very childhood
Here, was rooted.
And I understood
Why it was
That he had gifted me
That music box:

A house of wood
With velvet lining
And melancholy
Tune within.
It was not just for me -
It was for him.
When the lid
Is lifted,
A ballerina twirls
To *Lara's Theme*
Which sings
Of long lost hills,
And frozen lands
Awaiting Spring.
I have it still.

All of that was long ago.
But in my dreams,
I am free to go
When I so please;
And all appears
Quite vividly:
The fir trees
And the lake below;
The *chata*
On the hillside slope;
And through the door:
The pine interior
And lamp of paraffin
Gently burning.
The old familiar faces
And much-loved spaces;
Laughter and singing;
Merry-making.
Walls filled
With memories
Forever enduring.

We had a weekend house
In Moravia.
On a tree-topped hillside
Overlooking a reservoir.

IRON CURTAIN

Back to the land
Of our father
We came:
To Moravia,
In Czechoslovakia.
To the neat
Bungalows
Of his childhood street;
And to relations in
The functional
Apartments
Of 'modernist' living
In the town
Of Hodonín;
Then to the relatives
In the villages,
And their small-holdings
Of vegetables
And fruit trees.

In this region,
Far from the capital,
Dwelt a people
Warm and hospitable.
The lush countryside
Flourished
With a beauty
Verdant and fertile.
Folk music and
Home-made wine -
Defining features
Of the Moravian
Way of life -
Saw its inhabitants
Through hard times.

There was little crime:
A freedom of sorts,
At least from
The sordid reports
Of the newspapers
Back home.
Here, we children could
Safely go wandering
Unchaperoned,
Amidst streets free
From litter and graffiti
And other evils
Unworthy
Of mentioning.
Freedom can be
A relative thing.

Time seemed stuck
In the past,
Far back,
Long lost.
But despite hardship,
There was strength
Of friendship;
And kinship;
And a zest
For living.
One felt it,
Bubbling and real,
Insuppressible:
An existence
Unparalleled
And exquisite
Beneath the surface
Of oppression which,
Far from stamping it out,
Seemed to intensify it.

The shops had few products,
And no branding;
But there was a naive charm
We found welcoming.
I remember
The aroma
Of coffee roasting,
And tobacco
And wood smoke
And rye bread,
All mingling
On entering
The grocery store,
Or *obchod,*
Which,
Due to the lack of
Advertising,
Was more like
Stepping through
Someone's front door.

I recall the toy shop,
Full to bursting
With things
Made in Czechoslovakia,
Unfindable elsewhere.
How at *Bata*'s
We were measured up
For a smart new pair
Of school shoes
For the coming year;
And in the department store,
How we gazed in awe
At the elegant tableware
In fine porcelain,
And crystal
From Bohemia.

The evils of the regime
No doubt escaped me then,
Too young to understand
The implications
And outrage.
The short-lived promise
Of Prague Spring:
Dubček's great compromise
In 'the human face'
Of communism' -
And the subsequent
Shock invasion.
The protest suicide
Of Jan Palach,
Who set himself alight
And died,
Engulfed in flames.
The shame
Etched on
Russian faces.

But to note
Dad's sad countenance
On leaving his homeland,
It was clear that
In England,
Nor had he found
Fulfilment.
Such extremes between
East and West,
Each with its own
Shortcomings -
Neither, best.
Here: the rat race
And breakdown
Of community;
The main measure of value,
Not friendship, but money.

There: a backward pace
And shortages,
Amongst other affronts;
The restriction
Of movements
And risk
Of imprisonment.

Yet,
Hidden in plain sight -
Bound in loyalty
And self-sufficiency,
Hearty home-cooking
And good company;
Weekends spent
In wood cabins
In the country;
Music and singing -
This life in Moravia,
Had a *Shangri-La*
Quality.

Perhaps,
Though more was
The shame for it,
The restrictions might,
Ironically,
Have preserved it.
At any rate,
We have never since
Re-found it.

Yes,
Freedom can be a thing
Most relative.

THE MEMORY OF WALLS

Far from empty
Are these four walls
Of bricks and mortar -
Don't be fooled.
Do you not feel
The life between?
The life within?
The life still living?
For what has passed
Has left its print,
Voices still whisper
And laughs still ring;
Impressions,
Lasting,
As surely as if
On the walls,
Were the writing,
I was here.
I was here.
I was here.

Those both living,
And departed,
Have left their mark
On these partitions:
Some dark;
Some light;
Some invisible;
Some in plain sight;
Portraits
And effects,
No longer here
And yet...
Passions;
Feelings; faces;
Things;

Cannot be effaced,
Cannot be effaced,
Cannot be effaced.

The childhood home,
Revisited once more,
After years of absence:
Taking a deep breath
I step through
The old front door,
Under the grey slate roof,
Onto the wood-plank floor -
Determined to be
Detached, aloof;
But the heart swells
In spite of itself
And remembers:
Here we ate,
And here we sat;
In this wall
Was a serving hatch.

I still hear the clatter
Of cutlery and plates;
The door slamming
Where the draught came in;
The front room fireplace
With coal-black stains;
In the breakfast room, a space
Where the Rayburn was once,
On which we made drop-scones.
Siblings squabbling,
Laughing,
Play-making,
Ghosts,
Ghosts,
Ghosts.

Here they all are
Safely bottled:
The old familiar
Creaks and noises,
Rustles and rattles:
Inerasable sounds
And voices,
Echoing
Echoing
Echoing.

For of course
I have never left this house:
The door closed behind
Me long ago;
But this place,
As if an old, familiar face,
Remains,
Reconstructed in my mind,
Clear, in all its details:
Every crevice,
Every nook,
Every cranny,
Carried with me.
And within:
Precious pieces
And memories imprinted
On the present,
Still existent;
Ready at each turn
To be awakened.

Mere bricks and mortar?
Never, never.
The walls remember.
They are
Immortal,
Immortal,
Immortal.

GOODBYE

Goodbye dear House
Goodbye front door,
Goodbye old path
That is much worn.

Goodbye front wall
And creaking gate
And latch which sticks
And makes one late.

For all your faults
You were our home:
It's curious how
We used to moan
But now
With fondness
Will recall,
Even these
When we are gone.

For time it is
To lock the door,
And hand the key
To someone new;
And hope they'll
Do their bit, as we,
To treat you well,
And with esteem.

That of a fine morn
They'll praise the view
And tend the garden,
Cut the lawn;
And tread with
Gentle footsteps on
The floorboards
Where we trod
'Ere long.

A prominent personage*
Once said,
It's right
That one should
Love one's home,
But not so much
It becomes
One's tomb.

And so, it's time,
We must move on.

We'll take some
Cuttings of the rose
And shrubs
And flowers
We loved the most.
And in due course
They'll thrive
And grow:
Reminders of
Our old sweet home.

So too,
Your walls
Will not forget
Things loved or lost,
And times, here spent.
For each of us
Will leave our print
Upon the places
Left behind
And we should strive
To do our best,
That posterity might
To us, be kind.

One last pause
At the old front gate
To take a photo
For memory's sake;

But even if
The picture fades,
Or to rack and ruin
You fall away,
For us forever
You'll remain,
Preserved
As we left you,
On this day.

Goodbye dear House,
Goodbye front door.
Goodbye old path
That is much worn.

---

*on a visit to Canterbury in 2020, we became 'accidental' pilgrims, wandering into the Dean's Chapel of the Cathedral and ending up by receiving a blessing. (The full significance of this can only be felt by those who have watched the 1940s Powell & Pressburger film, *A Canterbury Tale*). During the service I was struck by these words spoken by the Dean, (which I have paraphrased for poetic purposes), attributed to a former home secretary.

Author Note:

This poem was in part inspired by Robert Louis Stevenson's *Farewell to the Farm*, a long-time favourite. For this reason, what might be deemed slightly old-fashioned language has been employed; but it suits the poem's style and underlines the sense of nostalgia.

THE BRAMBLES

The brambles are coming.
Year by year
They have crept nearer,
Across the paddock.
Once the livestock
Had gone -
The cows, the goats -
There was nothing
Which could
Stop them.

They wound their way
Through the long grass,
Like snakes
With sharp teeth,
Venomous.
We did our best
To keep them down:
Hacking away;
Pulling
At impossible roots;
Burning the ground;
To no avail.

When we were young,
The brambles
Framed
Our childish play.
They leant against
The far boundary
Of the land,
In regular spirals,
Like barbed wire
With a central hollow
Through which,
Unharmed,
We burrowed.

The foliage without:
Bristling of stem,
And burgeoning
With promised fruit,
Concealed our den;
Its fragile flowers
Unfurled in
A delicate scattering
Of white and pink;
The ground beneath,
Earthy and safe, was
Well-worn and trod.

A few planks of wood
Made good the floor;
Marmite sandwiches
And orange squash,
An adequate lunch;
And blackberries,
In season,
Succulent,
And delicious,
Were free
For the taking.

But now,
The brambles
Are wild,
Un-child-friendly,
Savage things with claws;
Unyielding and injurious;
And the blackberries,
Once sweet
And generous in size -
Plentiful enough
For jam, and crumbles
And pies -
Are tart; unripening;
Worm-ridden;
Bitter.

The brambles
Have grown over
The entire field,
Malicious
And strangling;
Scratching;
Wounding.
And thoughts,
Full of spikes,
Treacherous
And tangled,
Fill the mind
With callow fruits
And unforgiving
Thorns.
And the bitter-sweet
Memory
Of what used to be
And is no more.

THE DOVES

It was the coo-ing
Of the doves
Which jolted me:
That muffled,
Throaty call,
Low and resonant,
Emanating from
The shrubbery.

An echoing
Reminiscent
Of the early walk
To school:
Down the hill
And past the copse
Where crows,
Over nests
In bare-branched
Trees,
Kept vigil.

That quiet mumble
Which yet carried far,
Beyond the screech
Of murderous
Crows;
Beyond the wood
And tangled
Undergrowth;
Towards our path
Along the road.
A warble soft
But guttural;
A throbbing,
Almost palpable,
Of smoothly-
Feathered
Throat.

I loved it then:
That early morning
Halloo
Which sent me
Into nonchalant
Reverie,
And lent
Happiness to
The onerous
Walk to school.
And which now -
Even to ears
Far less finely
Attuned -
Revives
That distant
Memory.

They were not doves,
To be precise,
But wood-pigeons:
Ungainly,
Gauche in flight,
And ruddier of hue;
But to me, who
Nursed worries
Which surprisingly
Can beset a child
Of tender years,
Always
They were doves:
Those gentle, kindly,
Harbingers
Of peace.

On that same path
Or others still,
To hear the familiar
Oo-ooo-oo,
Oo-oo,

Stirs my heart
Without fail:

I am at once
A child
Of eight again,
Absorbed
In daydream,
Beneath
A benevolent wing;
And all is well.

V
THE
EXTRAORDINARY
ORDINARY

Blessed are they who see beautiful things in humble places where other people see nothing

- Camille Pissarro

THE EXTRAORDINARY
ORDINARY
I

Take the time
To breathe in
The earthy smell
Of the ground
After the rain;

To marvel
Of a dewy morning,
At the starling's
Iridescent sheen
Of violet and green;

To sift through
Unhurried fingers,
The myriad pebbles
On the beach
Of shingle; each
Perfectly imperfect
And unique.

To watch with awe,
The glorious drama
Of thunderclouds
Gathering
Before the storm,
And the power
Of nature,
Which makes all else
Seem small;

And after:

To feel the warmth
Of the sun's rays
On one's face -
An embrace
Tender and chaste
Like no other.

In moments of
Quiet,
Take the time
To listen to
The poetry
Of life:

Every word
A window;
Every pattern,
A rhyme.

THE EXTRAORDINARY
ORDINARY
II

Dwell
For a while
On the extraordinary
Of the everyday:

On the mantel
Proudly displayed,
The much-loved books
And photos, framed.
Time capsules
Of thought and face;
Wisdom shared
In print on page.

The sunlight
As it streams in
Of a fine morning,
Falling upon
The objects
In its pathway -
Favourite things
Collected
Over years;
A home built
Piece by piece;
Remember
Where and when
You got them,
And all the reasons
Why you love them.

And in the rituals
Of the day-to-day:

That cup of tea
Which should be
A ceremony;
The family meal,
Which ought to be
Enjoyed with all
The accoutrements
Of glory -
Treasured pieces
Of generations
Past and present;
Life stories
Which never die,
And, in time,
Become legend.

The fragrant candle
Which should not
Gather dust,
But burn,
With fiery flame
And scent
Of bergamot,
Or musk.

That china,
Saved for best,
Which ought
To be used lest
Time slip away;
Because 'best'
Is now;
Right here;
Today.

EYE OF THE BEHOLDER

Learn to know
That beauty which,
Though aging,
Never will grow old:
Every line,
A story, told;
Every wrinkle,
A memory, etched;
Each dimple,
A well from which
Laughter is drawn.

To have compassion,
Too – yes, even for
The furrowed brow,
Which bears the marks
Of crosses, borne.
And fondness,
For the scars
Of courage met
And mettle, shown
In battles
Lost, or won;
And duels,
Fought at dawn,
For you.

Petals, unfolding;
Passion, holding.
Nectar, ever sweeter
Towards the centre.

May such a beauty,
In all its layers,
From youth
To maturity,
And such a love,
Across the years,
Be ours,
For eternity.

THANK YOU FOR THE PAGES

Thank you for the pages:
Paperback-plain,
Or bound in cloth
With colour plates.
Pages pored over
From an early age;
Devoured and revered;
Bookmarked;
Dog-eared.

Oh, the joy of time
Alone -
A glorious hour
In one's room;
Or in a library
Amidst honeyed wood,
Wishing time stood
Still a little longer:
If only I could read
Another line,
Another page,
Another chapter...

When I was young,
Evening would find me
Tucked beneath
An eiderdown
In the childhood
Boudoir,
Freezing cold
In winter,
With nothing but
A hot brick
From the Rayburn
To warm the feet -
And the Greats
Of literature
To sustain me.

That first page,
Scanned,
With eager scrutiny:
Will it pass muster?
Let's give it a chapter;
If it does, it becomes
A veritable
Bosom chum -
Un-put-down-able,
Jealously guarded;
And if borrowed,
Returned, oh how
Reluctantly.

The brooding backdrop
Of the Brontës:
Ordinary lives
Touched by
The extraordinary;
The wild moors
Brought to the reader's
Very door,
Stark and vivid;
The rain and wind,
Never depicted
More romantically,
Nor felt as keenly.

Pages which guided me
Around the very tips
Of danger:
Moonfleet and *Moonstone,*
Du Maurier, Defoe;
Stories steeped
In suspense
And mystery;
Unlocking
The past
Or venturing
Into the vast
Unknown.

In memoir:
The heart-rending
Recountings
Of Gorky,
Written with
Such poignancy
As to be strangely
Uplifting:
The gift of the raconteur,
And the human spirit,
Resilient,
Transcending
Raw existence.

And in poetry:
Passion,
Simmering,
Beneath the surface,
With powerful fragility;
Imprinting itself
Upon my brain,
Ingrained
In patterns, rhymes
And haunting refrain;
Ready to be drawn on,
Again
And again
And again.

Thank you
For the pages,
Classic
And ageless;
Pristine or faded;
Dear friends,
Revisited;
New friends
In the making.

In my ivory tower,
Safe from time
And tide
Receding,
There,
You'll find me
Of a quiet hour
Still,
In good company -
Reading.

GREEN, HOW I LOVE YOU, GREEN!

Green, how I love you, green!
In woodland glades
On burnt-edged days,
I have found you in
The dappled shade
Of leafy arbours;
And reflected in
Slow-moving rivers
From over-stretching arms
Of weeping willows;
And in gilt-framed
Mirrors:
Eyes of rare
Green sapphire,
Sparkling,
With secret fire.

Green,
I have found you in
The rippling swathes
Of waves of grass
On untrod paths;
The jade-tinged forms,
Washed up on shores,
Of sea-smoothed glass
On timeless stones.
And in the Hebrides
On mossy rocks
In hidden coves
At the edge
Of the world.

Green, how I love you, green,
In the dark of holly,
And damp skins
Of briny olives;
The soft, pale flesh
Of avocado,
And sculpted forms
Of *poires d'Anjou.*

And in the treasured
Sanctity
Of memory:
On larder shelves
In old Moravia
Laden with jars
Of pickled cucumber.

Green,
I have sought you
In the galleries
Of artists,
Long-departed;
And at Giverny,
In Green Harmony
Amidst the water lilies
Of Monet's gardens;
In the olive groves
Of Van Gogh's
Provence,
Viewed from
The monastery
Of St Rémy;
And have found,
As last,
Repose,
In the cool shadows
Of Pissarro's
Poplar trees.

Green,
I have seen you
In winter oceans'
Enigmatic deeps;
And in seaweed
Flung on shorelines
By the high tide's
Fast retreat;

In the Emerald Isle's
Verdant pastures -
Lands blessed
With poetry -
Where playwrights
Long have prospered
In long nights
Which never sleep.

Pour me then,
Your precious
Tincture
Of intoxicating
Absinthe,
That at the font
Of knowledge,
I might freely drink;
And that,
By waxy candlelight,
Pen poised
Above the page,
I might pay homage
To your image,
For of all colours,
You are Queen.

Green,
How I love you,
Green!

Inspired by Garcia Lorca's celebrated work, *Romance
Sonámbulo*, in the version translated from the Spanish by
Spender & Gili, of which the opening line is: *Green, how I
love you, Green.* [A closer translation is in fact Alan
Wheatley's version 'Green, how I want you, Green'.]

MARGARITA

The recipe
For a good margarita
Is no secret;
But it is an art
To achieve it.

The base note:

The exquisite essence
Of agave
From that exotic
Succulent
Of Mexico:
A shot of Tequila
Reposado,
Turned by alchemy
Of oak,
To liquid gold.

Next:

A half measure
Of triple-sec
For the aroma
Of oranges,
Sun-soaked;

And finally:

The fresh-pressed
Juice of limes -
A little less;
The citrus
Top note.

[Shake well with ice,
And serve on the rocks
With slice of lime]

So here you have
The Margarita:

A cocktail
Born,
Of scorching
Heat;
Its liquor,
Cradled
In oak barrels,
Which leave
Their legacy
Of earthy peat;

Picture,
Pitted orange-peels
Hung to dry
In Seville's
Bright sun;
And the glistening
Fruits
Of lime-trees,
Ripening,
In lands
Far-flung;

Savour,
Through the salted
Rim,
The prickly plant's
Divine bouquet;
Allow
To linger
On the taste-buds
The memory
Of bitter spines
And nectar,
Sweet;

Now drink,
At last,
From
The frosted glass,
This incomparable
Aperitif,
Spirits lifted
By the zest
Of lime,
In this sublime
Restorative.

VI
FINAL WORD

"Perhaps, already, there are many thinking as we do... Maybe there are already writers like us. But that doesn't matter... It's we who must do it!"

\- Hans Fallada, *Alone in Berlin*

-

BEYOND THE PALE

They said
It couldn't
Happen here -

That the masses
Might some day
Revere
The madman
Dressed
In the Emperor's
New clothes.

They said
The day would
Never come
When the lunatics
Would be
Allowed to run
The asylum;
And that madness
Would be
The new normal.

[*One flew over
the cuckoo's nest,
didn't you see?*]

We never thought
That freedom,
So hard fought for,
Could evaporate
Before our eyes;
Nor that Orwell's
Nineteen Eighty Four,
Might one day
Summarize
Our lives.

It takes true grit,
Make no mistake,
To wade against
The surging tide;
To wage war,
From on
The losing side;
Yes, even to be
The pariah.
But it is noble
And it is right.
Hold fast;
Do not blanch.

At least *you*
Will be able
To say that,
In your small way,
You tugged at
The scaffold
Of the lynch mobs;
Opposed
The trials
Without jury;
Exposed
The deniers
Of History.
That you can plead
Not guilty.

Letter by letter,
Word by word,
Spell out
The absurd.

*Who will send
The first postcard?* *

114

It is time
To part ways
With those
Sleep-walking
To their graves:
Lemmings, flocking
Unquestioningly
To cliff-top edges
And the end
Of days.

Stay wide awake.

Point out
The glaringly
Obvious;
Live on the fringes
If you must;
Find others
You can trust -
They are out there,
Somewhere.

The Truth
Is still
The Truth,
Even if you are in
A minority
Of one**

But take heart;
You are not alone.

---

* Referencing the actions of Otto and Anna Quangel in *Alone in Berlin*
(Hans Fallada) based on the true story of Otto and Elise Hampel.
** (i) Mahatma Gandhi
(ii) George Orwell, *1984:*
Being in a minority, even in a minority of one, did not make you
mad. There was truth and there was untruth, and if you clung to
the truth even against the whole world, you were not mad.

Index of First Lines

About the Author

The author was born in Canterbury, Kent and grew up in the semi-rural but bustling village of Charing. The childhood home, a solid, square, brick-built building set on an immense rockery, with pine-trees to one side and an old orchard, coppice and paddock at the rear, was situated on the outskirts of the village, high on a hill above the Pilgrim's Way. It was, then, and remains, a source of inspiration for much of her poetry.

After completing her primary and secondary education locally, the author went on to King's College London, graduating with First Class Honours in French with English. Having acquired along the way an equal fascination for Russian Literature, her writing has been influenced by Lermontov, Gorky, Camus, Fournier, and Shakespeare. But not more so than by her own experiences of a somewhat poignant childhood and the rich traditions of story-telling, song-writing, folklore, and poetry passed down from both the Czech and English sides of her parentage. In Part IV (*The Memory of Walls, Revisited*) two poems, *Weekend House* and *Iron Curtain*, are drawn directly from childhood and adolescent experiences of family visits to then-communist Czechoslovakia: these are, effectively, privileged eye-witness accounts of the era.

She has previously produced children's books for schools in parallel French and English text, and is currently completing a substantial work, *Mid-Century Modern on a Shoestring & The Memory of Walls* which combines her love of interiors with her love of poetic prose.

The author is married, has two almost-grown-up daughters, and lives near the sea in Devon.

About the Illustrator

Isabella Synek Herd is the author's daughter, currently reading Architecture at Cambridge. Impassioned by post-war modernism and 1940s film, her interests in the art of the era and neo-romanticism are expressed admirably in her pen & ink illustrations especially executed for *Beyond the Pale*.

Also available in poetry:

The Memory of Walls
by Jana Synková

Printed in Great Britain
by Amazon